Lindsey Vonn

ABDO
Publishing Company

Vancouver 2010
16

by Sarah Tieck

VISIT US AT
www.abdopublishing.com

Published by ABDO Publishing Company, 8000 West 78th Street, Edina, Minnesota 55439.

Copyright © 2011 by Abdo Consulting Group, Inc. International copyrights reserved in all countries. No part of this book may be reproduced in any form without written permission from the publisher. Big Buddy Books™ is a trademark and logo of ABDO Publishing Company.

Printed in the United States of America, North Mankato, Minnesota.
052010
092010

 PRINTED ON RECYCLED PAPER

Coordinating Series Editor: Rochelle Baltzer
Contributing Editors: Heidi M.D. Elston, Megan M. Gunderson, BreAnn Rumsch, Marcia Zappa
Graphic Design: Maria Hosley
Cover Photograph: *AP Photo*: Gero Breloer.
Interior Photographs/Illustrations: *AP Photo*: Giovanni Auletta (pp. 19, 29), Nathan Bilow (p. 23), Luca Bruno (pp. 5, 21), Stefeno Dall'Ara (p. 20), Paul Drinkwater/NBCU Photo Bank via AP Images (p. 26), Frank Gunn, CP (p. 25), Thomas Kienzle (p. 15), Charles Krupa (p. 16), Kurt Menshing/The Mining Journal (p. 11), Armando Trovati (pp. 7, 19, 23); *Getty Images*: Brian Bahr/ALLSPORT (p. 9), DON EMMERT/AFP (p. 15); *iStockphoto*: ©iStockphoto.com/Adventure_Photo (p. 13).

Library of Congress Cataloging-in-Publication Data

Tieck, Sarah, 1976-
  Lindsey Vonn : Olympic champion / Sarah Tieck.
    p. cm. -- (Big buddy biographies)
  ISBN 978-1-61613-978-0
  1. Vonn, Lindsey--Juvenile literature. 2. Skiers--United States--Biography--Juvenile literature. I. Title.
  GV854.2.V66T54 2011
  796.93'5092--dc22
  [B]
                         2010013515

Lindsey
Vonn

Contents

Olympic Star

Lindsey Vonn is a famous skier. She has more World Cup wins than any other American skier. She is also the first American woman to win an Olympic gold **medal** in downhill. Lindsey is one of the world's best downhill ski racers!

⑤

Did you know...

Downhill ski racing is also called Alpine ski racing. Lindsey skis in five types of races. They are slalom, giant slalom, super-G, downhill, and combined.

Family Ties

Lindsey Kildow was born in St. Paul, Minnesota, on October 18, 1984. Her parents are Linda Krohn and Alan Kildow. Lindsey has two younger sisters and two younger brothers. They are Karin, Laura, Reed, and Dylan.

Lindsey's parents helped their daughter become a strong skier.

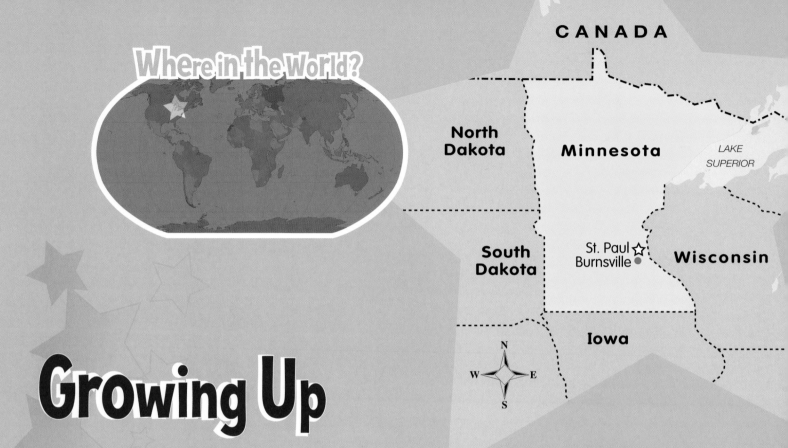

CANADA

North Dakota

Minnesota

LAKE SUPERIOR

South Dakota

St. Paul
Burnsville

Wisconsin

Iowa

N
W E
S

Growing Up

Lindsey grew up in Burnsville, Minnesota. Linda had a **stroke** during Lindsey's birth. Even after recovering, she faced many **challenges** during Lindsey's childhood.

Lindsey's family lived near a ski hill called Buck Hill. Alan had been a ski racer. He taught Lindsey to ski there when she was about three years old.

Lindsey says her mother's courage taught her to work hard.

At Buck Hill, Lindsey began working with ski **coach** Erich Sailer. He taught her to ski fast! Lindsey's dad noticed her talent. He believed one day she could **compete** in the Olympics.

By age seven, Lindsey began traveling so she could also ski during the summer. Two years later, Erich took her to Europe to give her a **challenge**.

Erich was Lindsey's first coach. He also coached Lindsey's dad. Erich is a well-known ski coach from Austria.

Did you know...

It became hard for Lindsey to attend a regular school because of ski practice and events. So in Vail, she was homeschooled. Lindsey learned from private teachers at home and while traveling.

Big Break

Lindsey needed to practice skiing on mountains to build her skills. When she was about 11, her parents decided to move the family to Vail, Colorado. There, Lindsey attended Ski Club Vail. This is a well-known winter sports school.

When Lindsey was 14, her hard work began to pay off. She won Italy's Trofeo Topolino competition. Lindsey was the first American woman to do this!

Vail is known for its large ski slopes.

13

The Olympic Games

At age 17, Lindsey **competed** in the 2002 Winter Olympics in Salt Lake City, Utah. Only the world's most skilled **athletes** compete in Olympic events.

Lindsey competed in two events. She took sixth place in combined. Lindsey placed higher than any other American female skier that year.

Lindsey became friends with famous ski racer Picabo Street (*right*) at the 2002 Olympics. Lindsey had first met Picabo when she was ten years old. She asked for Picabo's autograph!

15

Lindsey often talks to reporters about her skiing.

Did you know...

Lindsey may go as fast as 85 miles (137 km) per hour on a ski hill! That is faster than most cars drive on a highway!

Famous Athlete

Lindsey became known for skiing at high speeds. She was also known for having strong skills in many different races.

Soon after turning 20, Lindsey won her first World Cup race. It took place in Lake Louise, Alberta, Canada. Lindsey would go on to win many more World Cup races.

Unusual Prizes

After winning a World Cup race in France, Lindsey was awarded a cow. Most winners trade their cows for prize money. But, Lindsey kept hers! It was named Olympe.

Olympe had calves named Sunny and Karin. Sunny had a calf, too. Now, Lindsey has several cows as well as a prize goat. They live on her friend's farm in Kirchberg, Austria.

The FIS Alpine Ski World Cup is a yearly event. Skiers from around the world compete. Title winners get globe-shaped trophies.

World Cup race winners often receive money, animals, or other gifts.

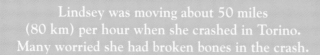

Lindsey was moving about 50 miles (80 km) per hour when she crashed in Torino. Many worried she had broken bones in the crash.

Turning Point

In 2006, Lindsey went to the Olympics for the second time. That year, the games were in Torino, Italy. Lindsey wanted to win a **medal** there.

But during practice, Lindsey crashed while skiing very fast. Many thought she was too hurt to ski again. When doctors said she was okay, Lindsey decided to race. She didn't win, but she was proud to have tried and done her best.

At the 2006 Olympics, Lindsey competed in the downhill, the super-G, and the slalom.

Olympic Friends

Lindsey has made friends with other skiers while **competing** around the world. One of her best friends is German skier Maria Riesch. Lindsey often spends Christmas with Maria's family in Germany.

Lindsey met U.S. skier Thomas Vonn at the 2002 Winter Olympics. They became close. Lindsey and Thomas married on September 29, 2007. They live in Park City, Utah.

Lindsey (*left*) and Maria (*right*) often compete against each other. But because they are friends, they also help each other. They share ideas and tips to race better.

Thomas and Lindsey both love to ski. He helps her improve her skiing skills.

23

Vancouver 2010

Lindsey's gold medal was for the downhill race. She got a bronze for the super-G.

By 2010, Lindsey had become a famous skier. She'd won two World Cup overall **titles**! Lindsey hoped to win her first gold **medal** at the 2010 Olympics in Vancouver, British Columbia, Canada.

During a training run in Austria, Lindsey hurt her leg. Some thought she wouldn't be able to race in the Olympics. But, Lindsey raced and won her first gold medal! She also won a bronze medal. Later, she continued to **compete** even after she broke her finger.

Did you know...

Lindsey is almost six feet (2 m) tall!

In March 2010, Lindsey talked about the Olympics when she appeared on *The Tonight Show with Jay Leno.*

26

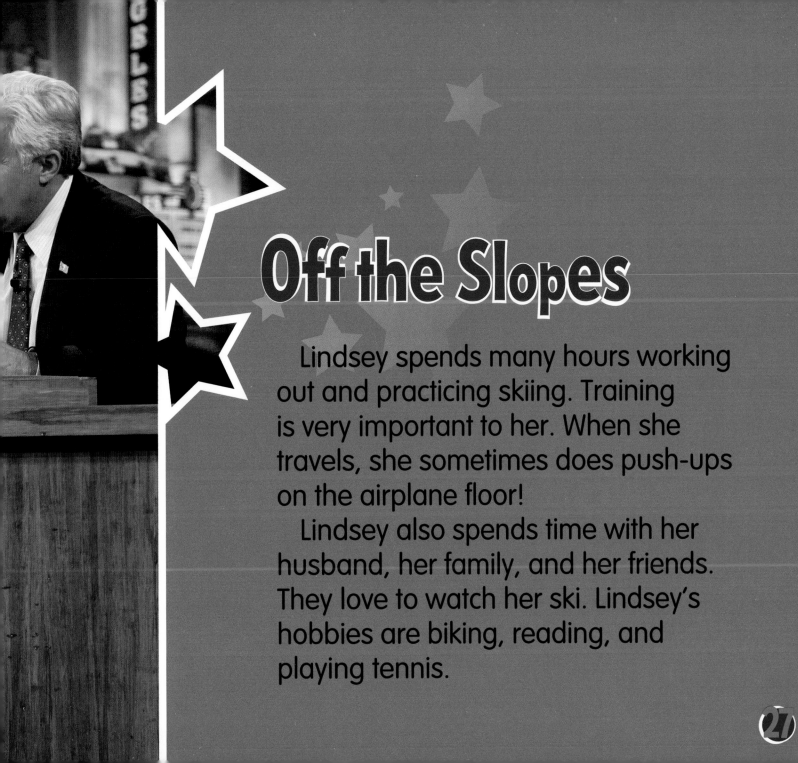

Off the Slopes

Lindsey spends many hours working out and practicing skiing. Training is very important to her. When she travels, she sometimes does push-ups on the airplane floor!

Lindsey also spends time with her husband, her family, and her friends. They love to watch her ski. Lindsey's hobbies are biking, reading, and playing tennis.

Buzz

Lindsey's fame continues to grow. In 2010, she won her third World Cup overall **title**! She's hoping to win a fourth one in 2011. And, she has started preparing for the 2014 Olympics in Russia.

Fans are excited to see what's next for Lindsey Vonn. Many believe she has a bright **future**!

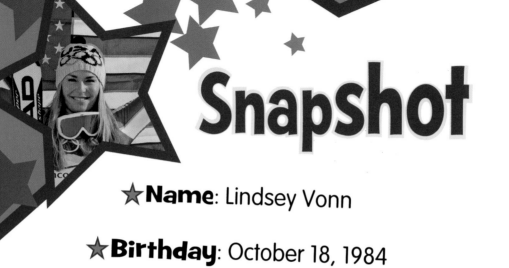

Snapshot

⭐**Name**: Lindsey Vonn

⭐**Birthday**: October 18, 1984

⭐**Birthplace**: St. Paul, Minnesota

⭐**Olympic medals won**: 1 gold, 1 bronze

Important Words

athlete a person who is trained or skilled in sports.

challenge (CHA-luhnj) something that tests one's strength or abilities.

coach someone who teaches or trains a person or a group on a certain subject or skill.

competition (kahm-puh-TIH-shuhn) a contest between two or more persons or groups. To compete is to take part in a competition.

future (FYOO-chuhr) a time that has not yet occurred.

medal an award for success.

stroke a medical problem caused by lack of blood flow to the brain. Strokes are serious. They may cause brain damage or death.

title a first-place position in a contest.

Web Sites

To learn more about Lindsey Vonn, visit ABDO Publishing Company online. Web sites about Lindsey Vonn are featured on our Book Links page. These links are routinely monitored and updated to provide the most current information available.

www.abdopublishing.com

Index